MERRILY Model

7 **Highly Effective Tools That Enhance Your Child's Speech-Language Development**

Paulette Y. Robinson, M.A. CCC-SLP

Illustrations by Denis Proulx, and inspired by Kathleen Y. Robinson

Library of Congress Cataloging-In-Publication Data

Robinson, Paulette Y.

MERRILY Model: 7 highly effective tools that enhance your child's speech-language development / by Paulette Y. Robinson
        p. cm.

ISBN: 1453752897
ISBN-13: 9781453752890
LCCN: 2010915000

This book is dedicated
to
Mia, Logan, Liam
and
all God's children.

TABLE OF CONTENTS

NOTE TO THE READER

The goal of this guidebook is to provide an easy, fun and effective guide for parents and caregivers to constructively support their child's speech-language development.

As a speech-language pathologist, I have treated and evaluated over a thousand children and I have come to realize that:

Children have a strong desire to learn and instinctively want to please.

You may feel overwhelmed with your child's speech-language development, especially if your child is showing delays in talking. With that in mind I designed MERRILY Model to be an easy, fun and effective tool to assist with your child's speech-language development. It is my passion to be that "helping hand" for you in your journey.

MERRILY Model are tools to ensure you use all of the available techniques together. The tools are easy to remember so you can apply them consistently each day, several times throughout the day. I want MERRILY Model to be a happy approach as you work to enhance your child's speech-language development.

The characters, Mary and Lee, will steer you through this guidebook. I will alternately refer to a child's gender with a masculine or feminine pronoun to avoid using "he or she" and "him or her."

The appendix in the back of the book provides additional resources to help you journal your child's success.

Paulette Y. Robinson

INTRODUCTION

Do you remember "Row, Row, Row Your Boat," the popular nursery rhyme and song?

> Row, row, row your boat,
> gently down the stream.
> MERRILY, merrily, merrily, merrily,
> life is but a dream.

Like the song, you want your child's speech-language development to be a gentle flow. It may start with a few splashes and ripples of language and then progress into waves and tides of communication as her skills advance. Each child's journey is unique, so be patient and "row gently" with the current.

HOW IT BEGINS

Speech is how we communicate our thoughts and emotions. Language is the set of shared rules that allows us to exchange those ideas or feelings through talking, gesturing or writing.

Let's compare watching a balloon inflate to watching your child's speech-language develop. When you inflate an ordinary balloon, it takes on the standard shape that all the other balloons have. If you look closely, you can see that each balloon has a unique way that it has taken shape. Often the difference is barely noticeable. The equivalent is true for your child's speech-language development. Overall, the development appears the same, but your child's speech-language is unique and is individually shaped by his internal and external environment. Sometimes the differences are very subtle.

Your child's speech-language development does not grow as quickly as an inflatable balloon. While you can observe the expansion of a balloon's growth, your child's expansion can be very subtle and it may take awhile before you can distinguish the changes.

Remember that each child is unique and that the following guidelines are generic for specific age groups. Consult with your child's speech-language pathologist or pediatrician if you have specific concerns.

There are two types of speech-language skills:

    (1) listening and understanding (receptive)

    (2) talking (expressive)

Listening and understanding are skills that we need to receive communication, and talking is how we express our thoughts and feelings to others.

Listening &
Understanding

Talking

Let us look at the common speech-language development milestones of children ages three and under. Included is a list of listening and understanding skills and talking skills for each age group.

Typical speech and language development (n.d.) Available from the website of the American Speech-Language-Hearing Association: http://www.asha.org/public/speech/development/).

SPLASHES

(Ages 0-6 Months)

Our first method of communicating with the world is crying. During the first few weeks of life, your baby will cry when he is uncomfortable. Feeling uncomfortable can be caused by hunger, a wet diaper, sleepiness, or any other reason your baby feels unhappy.

As your baby grows, his speech-language skills are growing as he listens and observes his environment. He will begin to coo and make sounds. You can stimulate your baby's speech-language development by providing an assortment of sounds, like playing music, talking, reading, and singing to him.

Your child's speech and language will progress from cooing to babbling. Encourage your child's language by playing with him and calling his name often when you speak to him. He will laugh and smile. Repeat his sounds back to him so you can encourage him to continue.

SPLASHES CHECKLIST

Listening and understanding skills

- ☐ Recognizes familiar voices
- ☐ Smiles at friendly voices
- ☐ Looks at your face when you talk
- ☐ Responds to loud noises
- ☐ Looks around in the direction of a sound

Talking skills

- ☐ Cries differently for specific needs
- ☐ Makes noise when spoken to
- ☐ Makes sounds when comfortable (cooing, raspberries, babbling)
- ☐ Reacts when happy (laughs, giggles) or unhappy (cries, fusses)

RIPPLES

(Ages 7-12 Months)

As your baby progresses, his babbling will begin to sound like he is really talking. He will say "ma-ma," "da-da," and other two syllable sounds that resemble words. In the beginning, he may not associate these sounds with anyone or anything, but eventually he will begin to understand more. He understands brief commands like "no-no." He will shake his head *no* and/or wave bye-*bye*.

You can stimulate your baby's speech-language development by playing games and singing songs. "Peek-a-boo," "This Little Piggy Went to Market," and other fun activities in various playful voice tones can expand your child's speech-language development.

Your child will begin to understand more and follow simple instructions like "give me the book." You may hear your child's first word. Learning an assortment of animal sounds, playing music, singing, and reading nursery rhymes and stories can encourage his speech-language development.

RIPPLES CHECKLIST

Listening and understanding skills

- ❐ Understands "no-no"
- ❐ Listens when spoken to
- ❐ Looks when you call his name
- ❐ Understands simple commands
- ❐ Comprehends a few words or phrases

Talking skills

- ❐ Laughs often
- ❐ Babbles with sounds like "ba-ba-ba" or "da-da-da"
- ❐ Attempts to imitate words
- ❐ Tries to talk with body language or gestures like pointing and waving
- ❐ Shouts to get your attention
- ❐ Sounds like he is talking, but not speaking real words
- ❐ Uses one to two words like "mama" and "dada"
- ❐ Begins to call out the name of familiar people or things

WAVES

(Ages 1-2 Years)

There is now an increase in your child imitating simple words. She can recognize the name of many familiar objects. Her pronunciation may be unclear, but she is attempting to name objects and people with two or three word phrases. She is also becoming more possessive and refers to objects as "Mine."

Your child enjoys someone reading to her. Her attention span with books or toys now lasts longer. Playing the same games, singing the same songs, and reading the same books help stimulate your child's speech-language development. "Patty-cake" and "Head, Shoulders, Knees and Toes" are interactive play that can encourage communication.

She can follow simple commands with gesture cues and later can follow your requests without gestures from you. She can identify her body parts. She can answer simple questions, like "Where is your ear?" and can point to her "ear" without you demonstrating.

WAVES CHECKLIST

Listening and understanding skills

- ☐ Listens to short stories being read
- ☐ Points to things, pictures, and familiar people
- ☐ Follows simple requests
- ☐ Points to body parts such as "nose"
- ☐ Comprehends basic action verbs like "drinking" and "sleeping"
- ☐ Understands about 200 words

Talking skills

- ☐ Asks for familiar foods by name
- ☐ Names objects and people in pictures
- ☐ Repeats animal sounds such as "moo" and "woof"
- ☐ Combines words such as "more juice"
- ☐ Begins to use possessive pronouns "mine" and "my"
- ☐ Says about 50+ words but may be mispronouncing some

TIDES

(Ages 2-3 Years)

Your child's speech-language (jargon) is beginning to become real word phrases. Sometimes, her pronunciation sounds jumbled because she is learning to coordinate her vocal muscles. Blowing soap bubbles is a fun way to exercise these muscles and improve coordination.

Your toddler now has a word label for most objects, people, and places she encounters. She may be leaving off the beginning or ending sounds on some words, yet you will understand your child's speech-language most of the time. She answers simple questions about familiar activities and is beginning to understand and follow a two-step command such as "get the ball and give it to me."

Your child can understand and express more concepts. She uses the plural forms of nouns such as "books" and "dogs" and the regular past tense of verbs like "looked." She distinguishes the difference between contrasts like "stop" and "go" and spatial positions such as "up," "down," or "under."

TIDES CHECKLIST

Listening and understanding skills

- ☐ Listens to longer stories being read
- ☐ Recognizes size concepts like "big" and "little"
- ☐ Comprehends locations like "under" and "on"
- ☐ Distinguishes pronouns such as "you," "me," and "her"
- ☐ Recognizes descriptive words such as "cold" and "hot"
- ☐ Understands most sentences directed to her
- ☐ Follows two-step directions
- ☐ Rapidly understands new words

Talking skills

- ☐ Begins to use more pronouns such as "you" and "I"
- ☐ Answers simple questions
- ☐ Uses a questioning voice inflection to ask for items, like "My toy?"
- ☐ Speaks in three to four word sentences
- ☐ Asks "what" and "where" questions
- ☐ Expresses negatives "no" and "not" in phrases
- ☐ Says about 300+ words correctly, but may mispronounce some

MARY & LEE

WHAT IS  MODEL?

MERRILY Model is 7 highly effective tools that enhance your child's speech-language development. The word "merrily" means cheerfully or happily. Happiness is what you want for your child. The word "merrily" will help you perform the tools that we want you to apply. Here is what each letter in MERRILY represents:

 **M**odeling

 **E**xpansion

 **R**epetition

 **R**einforcement

 Inquiry

 Labeling

 **Y**ou and Your Youngster

Each MERRILY Model tool focuses on a different concept, yet they all work together. MERRILY Model is a holistic approach and, therefore, the tools may overlap. Many of the actions you perform can address the development of multiple speech-language skills.

Let us define each tool in MERRILY Model. Keep in mind that your child's response will depend on her developmental level.

odeling is you demonstrating speech-language behavior or being a role model for your child to imitate.

For example, you are modeling correct pronunciation when Lee states "Wabbit," and you reply, "Yes, that is a rabbit."

Always model the sounds or words you would want Lee to imitate. Limit talking "baby talk" to your child, especially after the age of 7 months. You want your child to model correct pronunciation.

xpansion is gradually increasing your child's words, understanding, or actions to the next level of performance.

In the beginning Mary may just point and you will say, "Juice," to expand her speech-language from saying no words to one word.

If Mary points and says "Juice," you add another word and reply, "Get juice" or "Drink juice." You have now expanded the communication from one word to two words. It is not necessary to coerce your child to repeat the additional words in order for her to begin expanding her understanding.

epetition is saying and doing the same things again and again.

Mary and Lee enjoy listening to the same songs or books over and over again. They are prone to understand and say a word when they frequently hear it used in context.

einforcement is praise for positive speech-language behavior you want to encourage.

Encourage Mary when she performs positive behavior. Create a simple way to celebrate together. Here are different examples of reinforcement that can indicate a job well done:

- Playful phrases
  - "Very good, very good, yay!"
  - "Way to go!"
  - "Good job!"

- Fun cheer or sounds
  - "Two, four, six, eight, who do we appreciate?!"
  - "Ta-dah!"
  - "Hip-hip-hooray!"

- Gestures
  - smile
  - special handshake
  - high five
  - hug

- Celebratory dances

- Song refrains
  - "That's the way, uh-huh, uh-huh, I like it, uh-huh uh-huh."

- Combination of the above

Establishing a simple method of quickly praising your child for small progressive steps reinforces that your child recognizes your acknowledgment of their successes.

nquiry is asking questions appropriate for your child's level of speech-language development.

For example, asking Lee "What is this?" while holding a ball or pointing to a picture of a ball. After waiting 7 seconds, you can call out its name as "ball."

Questions can be indicated with inflections in voice or body language.

Encourage your child to reveal more by asking him open ended questions. Open ended questions are those that cannot be answered with just a yes or no response.

abeling is audibly stating the name of items or actions as they occur.

Initially, you will want to use single words to identify the name of objects, like saying "Book."

"Let's read a book." "Get the book." "Turn the page." "See the ball." These statements tell actions or identify items. Mary and Lee learn as they hear the labels in context of what is occurring.

ou and **Your Youngster** together are the most important components of all the tools for your child's speech-language development.

merrilymodel.com

Here are some actions you can take to strengthen your youngster's confidence and support him:

- Listen patiently as your youngster communicates.

- Give your youngster the time he needs to communicate his thoughts or emotions.

- Allow your youngster to speak; do not hurry to fill in missing or misused words.

- Always respond to your youngster's attempts to communicate.

- Praise your youngster's attempts at communication, whether successful or not.

- Position yourself at eye level when you communicate with your youngster.

- Present questions in their simplest form and in a positive format.

- Reward your youngster after a desired outcome.

- Practice blowing soap bubbles with your youngster. It is a fun way to exercise speech-language muscles and improve coordination.

- Speak slowly and clearly to your youngster.

- Turn off the television.

- Talk often to your youngster.

- Encourage verbal and nonverbal communication by providing at least two choices, such as "Do you want an apple or a cracker?"

- Use inflection while talking and singing to your youngster.

- Ask your youngster's speech-language therapists if there are activities you can engage in with your youngster.

- Keep a positive attitude for your youngster to model.

Now you have MERRILY Model to assist you with the tools that enhance your child's speech-language development. Use the 7 tools throughout your everyday activities until they flow naturally for you. Row your boat gently and log your child's progress.

 **M**odeling

 **E**xpansion

 **R**epetition

 **R**einforcement

 **I**nquiry

 **L**abeling

 **Y**ou and **Your Youngster**

OPTIMIZE THE OPPORTUNITY

MERRILY Model provides creative tools and stimulation techniques that are easy to apply and share with your child.

You can use MERRILY Model tools during daily and playtime activities to strengthen your child's confidence and support him. Below are activities identified in this guidebook which you can use to enhance your child's speech-language development:

Maximize that Moment

<u>(Daily Activities)</u>

- Getting dressed

- Brushing teeth

- Grooming hair

- Eating meals and snacks

- Fastening clothes

- Riding in a car

- Watching educational programs

- Shopping at the grocery store

Play with Purpose

<u>(Playtime Activities)</u>

    🔍 Playing with a box

    🔍 Playing with a toy

    🔍 Exploring books

    🔍 Singing songs

    🔍 Reciting nursery rhymes

    🔍 Playing with games

All of these opportunities can be optimized to elicit communication from your child throughout the day. How can Maximize that Moment and Play with Purpose enhance your child's speech-language development? When you perform these MERRILY Model tools in everyday situations with your child, you are encouraging her speech-language development.

MAXIMIZE THAT MOMENT

(Daily Activities)

Make the most of everyday tasks with your child to encourage her speech-language development.

Here are some daily activities that you can use to practice MERRILY Model.

Getting Dressed

Every morning while getting dressed, you have an opportunity to communicate with your child. Some topics to discuss while getting dressed:

- selecting outfits,
- recognizing colors,
- categorizing clothing items,
- identifying body parts that the clothing covers, and
- deciding the easiest way to put on the clothing items.

Talk aloud to your child while you are dressing yourself and her. Describe what you are doing, using an assortment of MERRILY Model tools for variety.

Let's focus on putting on shoes.

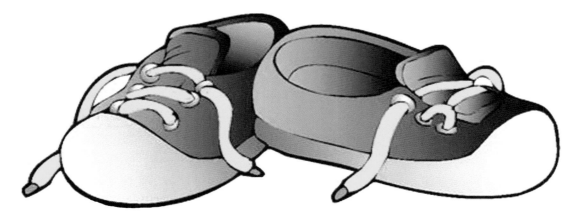

Your child's responses will depend on his developmental level. Encourage communication, but do not attempt to force it.

Remember, there will be overlap and repetition in your statements because you are communicating the same thing in various ways to optimize the opportunity. Each interaction can support the growth of more than one speech-language development.

Modeling:	"Let's put on your shoes. I have on my shoes. Fasten your shoes. I am tying my shoes."
Expansion:	"Shoes. My shoes. Mommy's shoes. Big shoes. Little shoes."
Repetition:	"Here is the shoe. There is a shoe. See the shoe. Get your shoe. Let's put on your shoes."
Reinforcement:	Look at your child and then smile. "Good job! You said shoes."
Inquiry:	"Where are your shoes? Did you find your shoes?"
Labeling:	"This is a shoe. Shoe? Yes, shoe. Let's put on your shoes."
You and Your Youngster:	Talk directly to your child throughout any activity. Use your child's name as you speak.

Now, it is time for you to practice applying MERRILY Model to many of your child's daily activities. The following pages will provide you with the opportunity to practice MERRILY Model.

Brushing Teeth

Brushing Teeth

For this activity, write interactions you can perform with your child for each MERRILY Model tool.

Modeling:	_____ _____
Expansion:	_____ _____
Repetition:	_____ _____
Reinforcement:	_____ _____
Inquiry:	_____ _____
Labeling:	_____ _____
You and Your Youngster:	_____ _____

"I learned the way a monkey learns - by watching its parents." ~ Prince Charles

Grooming Hair (combing, brushing, washing)

Grooming Hair (combing, brushing, washing)

For this activity, write interactions you can perform with your child for each MERRILY Model tool.

Modeling:	
Expansion:	
Repetition:	
Reinforcement:	
Inquiry:	
Labeling:	
You and Your Youngster:	

"I will act as if what I do will make a difference." ~ William James

Eating Meals and Snacks

For this activity, write interactions you can perform with your child for each MERRILY Model tool.

 **M**odeling:	_____ _____
Expansion:	_____ _____
Repetition:	_____ _____
Reinforcement:	_____ _____
Inquiry:	_____ _____
Labeling:	_____ _____
You and Your Youngster:	_____ _____

"Never discourage anyone...who continually makes progress, no matter how slow." ~ Plato

Fastening Clothing

Fastening Clothing

For this activity, write interactions you can perform with your child for each MERRILY Model tool.

Modeling:	_____ _____
Expansion:	_____ _____
Repetition:	_____ _____
Reinforcement:	_____ _____
Inquiry:	_____ _____
Labeling:	_____ _____
You and Your Youngster:	_____ _____

"An investment in knowledge always pays the best interest." ~ Benjamin Franklin

Riding in a Car

Riding in a Car

For this activity, write interactions you can perform with your child for each MERRILY Model tool.

Modeling:	_____ _____
Expansion:	_____ _____
Repetition:	_____ _____
Reinforcement:	_____ _____
Inquiry:	_____ _____
Labeling:	_____ _____
You and Your Youngster:	_____ _____

"The way positive reinforcement is carried out is more important than the amount."
~ B. F. Skinner

Watching Educational Programs

Television should be supervised, educational, and timed according to the child's developmental age.

Watching Educational Programs

For this activity, write interactions you can perform with your child for each MERRILY Model tool.

Modeling:	_____ _____
Expansion:	_____ _____
Repetition:	_____ _____
Reinforcement:	_____ _____
Inquiry:	_____ _____
Labeling:	_____ _____
You and Your Youngster:	_____ _____

"Almost anything can become a learning experience if there is enough caring involved."
~ Mary MacCracken

Shopping at the Grocery Store

Shopping at the Grocery Store

For this activity, write interactions you can perform with your child for each MERRILY Model tool.

Modeling:	_____ _____
Expansion:	_____ _____
Repetition:	_____ _____
Reinforcement:	_____ _____
Inquiry:	_____ _____
Labeling:	_____ _____
You and Your Youngster:	_____ _____

"The beautiful thing about learning is that no one can take it away from you." ~ B.B. King

PLAY WITH PURPOSE

(Playtime Activities)

Playtime provides the same opportunity to elicit communication from your child as other daily tasks. When you play with your child with the intent to encourage his speech-language development, you are playing with purpose.

The following examples show how to practice MERRILY Model while playing.

Safety First

It's important to use age appropriate toys and games that are safe for your child. Ensure that any toy or object is clean and free of hazardous elements. Remove any item that consists of material your child could swallow.

Playing with a Box

In addition to toys, your child often explores and plays with household items. For example, Mary enjoys playing with empty containers, pots, and pans. Let us explore how we can apply MERRILY Model when Mary is playing with a box.

Remember your child's responses will depend on her developmental level. Encourage communication, but do not attempt to force it.

Modeling:	Point to the box and say, "Box." Your child may imitate you. Place your hand or a smaller toy inside the box and say, "Put the toy (or "your hand") in the box. The toy is in the box." Remove the toy and say, "Take the toy out of the box. The toy is out of the box."
Expansion:	"Box. Get box. Empty box. Big box. Your toy box."
Repetition:	"Box, Box, Here is the box. See the box. Get the box."
Reinforcement:	Look at your child and then smile. "You found the box!"
Inquiry:	"What is this? Box? What is in the box? Where is the box?"
Labeling:	"This is a box. Box? Yes, box. Let's put Baby in the box."
You and Your Youngster:	Talk directly to your child while you play and call your child by name. Have fun.

Remember, there will be overlap and repetition in your statements because you are communicating the same thing in various ways to optimize the opportunity. Each interaction can support the growth of more than one speech-language development.

Playing with a Toy

Let us look at some examples of how to apply MERRILY Model to a toy such as a Jack-in-the-box.

Modeling:	Demonstrate verbally how to play with the Jack-in-the-box. While Jack is enclosed in the box, crank the handle until Jack pops out. Express surprise and show your child how to push Jack back in the box and close the lid. Repeat and let your child do it if he is able and interested.
Expansion:	"Jack. Jack in. Jack out."
Repetition:	"Jack, Jack, Here is Jack. See Jack. Get Jack."
Reinforcement:	Look at your child, laugh, and clap. "Yay, it is Jack-in-the-box!"
Inquiry:	"What is this? Jack-in-the-box? What is in the box? Where is Jack?"
Labeling:	"This is Jack-in-the-box. Jack is in the box. Turn the handle. Let us put Jack back in the box."
You and Your Youngster:	Call your child's name when talking to him. Give your child the time he needs to communicate his thoughts or emotions.

Now, it is time for you to practice applying MERRILY Model to some ordinary playtime activities your child enjoys. The following pages will provide you with the opportunity to continue practicing MERRILY Model.

Exploring Picture Books

For this activity, write interactions you can perform with your child for each MERRILY Model tool.

Modeling:	
Expansion:	
Repetition:	
Reinforcement:	
Inquiry:	
Labeling:	
You and Your Youngster:	

"Accumulate learning by study; understand what you learn by questioning."
~ Cha'n Master Mingjiao

Singing Songs

For this activity, write interactions you can perform with your child for each MERRILY Model tool.

Modeling:	_____ _____
Expansion:	_____ _____
Repetition:	_____ _____
Reinforcement:	_____ _____
Inquiry:	_____ _____
Labeling:	_____ _____
You and Your Youngster:	_____ _____

"Repetition is the mother of learning." ~ White Mountain Apache Indians Archives

Reciting Nursery Rhymes

Reciting Nursery Rhymes

For this activity, write interactions you can perform with your child for each MERRILY Model tool.

Modeling:	_____ _____
Expansion:	_____ _____
Repetition:	_____ _____
Reinforcement:	_____ _____
Inquiry:	_____ _____
Labeling:	_____ _____
You and Your Youngster:	_____ _____

"It is the supreme art of the teacher to awaken joy in creative expression and knowledge." ~ Albert Einstein

Playing with Games

Playing with Games

For this activity, write interactions you can perform with your child for each MERRILY Model tool.

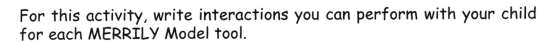odeling:	_____ _____
xpansion:	_____ _____
epetition:	_____ _____
einforcement:	_____ _____
nquiry:	_____ _____
abeling:	_____ _____
ou and Your Youngster:	_____ _____

"Wherever you are, be there." ~ Ralph Waldo Emerson

SUMMARY

Remember that your interactions with your child and your comments to your child will be repeated often. The daily and playtime activities of life are very repetitive. Would you stop watering your plants because you could not see their daily growth?

Over time, the growth in your child's speech-language development will become noticeable. You are communicating the same thing in various ways to "Optimize the Opportunity." Every contact supports the development of multiple speech-language skills, so remain patient. Continue to use the 7 tools of MERRILY Model each day. For your convenience, the 7 tools for enhancing your child's speech-language development are provided in the appendix. Perform them frequently each day to "Maximize that Moment" and "Play with Purpose."

APPENDIX

The following resources are included in this appendix to continue supporting your participation in your child's speech-language development:

MERRILY Model Summary is a review of the 7 highly effective tools that enhance your child's speech-language development.

Practice Activity Sheets are additional sheets for your use to plan how you will apply the MERRILY Model in new activities with your child that may not have been previously discussed.

Congratulations certificate is to acknowledge your completion of the practice activities in this guide book and a reminder to continue practicing your skills with your child.

Progress Log is your personal record to monitor the progress you observe in your child's speech-language development over time. Use the log as often as you like to write down changes you notice in your child's speech-language development and share it with your speech-language professional.

Model Summary

Modeling:	You demonstrating speech-language behavior or being a role model for your child to imitate.
Expansion:	Gradually increasing your child's words, understanding, or actions to the next level of performance.
Repetition:	Saying and doing the same things again and again.
Reinforcement:	Praise for positive speech-language behavior you want to encourage.
Inquiry:	Asking questions appropriate for your child's level of speech-language development.
Labeling:	Audibly stating the name of items or actions as they occur.
You and Your Youngster:	Together these are the most important components of all the tools for your child's speech-language development.

Practice Activity Sheet

Practice Activity: _____

For this activity you have selected, write interactions you can perform with your child for each MERRILY Model tool.

Modeling:	_____ _____
Expansion:	_____ _____
Repetition:	_____ _____
Reinforcement:	_____ _____
Inquiry:	_____ _____
Labeling:	_____ _____
You and Your Youngster:	_____ _____

"A smile is a language that even a baby understands."

Practice Activity Sheet

Practice Activity: _____

For this activity you have selected, write interactions you can perform with your child for each MERRILY Model tool.

Modeling:	_____ _____
Expansion:	_____ _____
Repetition:	_____ _____
Reinforcement:	_____ _____
Inquiry:	_____ _____
Labeling:	_____ _____
You and Your Youngster:	_____ _____

"A smile is a language that even a baby understands."

Practice Activity Sheet

Practice Activity: _____

For this activity you have selected, write interactions you can perform with your child for each MERRILY Model tool.

Modeling:	_____ _____
Expansion:	_____ _____
Repetition:	_____ _____
Reinforcement:	_____ _____
Inquiry:	_____ _____
Labeling:	_____ _____
You and Your Youngster:	_____ _____

"A smile is a language that even a baby understands."

Practice Activity Sheet

Practice Activity: _____

For this activity you have selected, write interactions you can perform with your child for each MERRILY Model tool.

Modeling:	_____ _____
Expansion:	_____ _____
Repetition:	_____ _____
Reinforcement:	_____ _____
Inquiry:	_____ _____
Labeling:	_____ _____
You and Your Youngster:	_____ _____

"A smile is a language that even a baby understands."

Practice Activity Sheet

Practice Activity: _____

For this activity you have selected, write interactions you can perform with your child for each MERRILY Model tool.

Modeling:	_____ _____
Expansion:	_____ _____
Repetition:	_____ _____
Reinforcement:	_____ _____
Inquiry:	_____ _____
Labeling:	_____ _____
You and Your Youngster:	_____ _____

"A smile is a language that even a baby understands."

Practice Activity Sheet

Practice Activity: _____

For this activity you have selected, write interactions you can perform with your child for each MERRILY Model tool.

Modeling:	_____ _____
Expansion:	_____ _____
Repetition:	_____ _____
Reinforcement:	_____ _____
Inquiry:	_____ _____
Labeling:	_____ _____
You and Your Youngster:	_____ _____

"A smile is a language that even a baby understands."

Congratulations!

_____

[Name of Parent or Caregiver]

has completed the practice activities in

Model

7 Highly Effective Tools That Enhance Your Child's Speech-Language Development

_____

[Date]

Progress Log

Whenever you practice MERRILY Model, log the date and behavior observed to track your child's progress. Track progress as often as the child's progress unfolds.

Date   Behavior Observed

_____   _____

_____   _____

_____   _____

_____   _____

_____   _____

_____   _____

_____   _____

_____   _____

_____   _____

_____   _____

_____   _____

_____   _____

_____   _____

_____   _____

_____   _____

Date

Behavior Observed

_____   _____

_____   _____

_____   _____

_____   _____

_____   _____

_____   _____

_____   _____

_____   _____

_____   _____

_____   _____

_____   _____

_____   _____

_____   _____

_____   _____

_____   _____

_____   _____

_____   _____

ABOUT THE AUTHOR

Paulette Y. Robinson, M.A. CCC-SLP/L

Paulette is the owner and clinical director of PYR Services, LLC. She has over 15 years of experience working in the field of Speech-language Pathology. She earned her bachelor's degree from Texas Southern University and her master's degree from Hampton University in Communication Science and Disorders. She is licensed in Illinois and is certified by the American Speech-Language-Hearing Association (ASHA).

Over 10 years ago, Paulette began working exclusively with children specifically and that's where she found her "true calling." She understands the importance and benefits of early identification and intervention when there are speech-language development issues in children. Because of this passion, Paulette developed PYR Services, LLC, whose mission is to reach more children and provide them with appropriate speech-language services.

Paulette conducts workshops where she uses a holistic approach to empower and educate parents and caregivers in techniques that enhance speech-language development in children.

For more information, please visit www.merrilymodel.com or www.pyrservices.com.

THANK YOU!!

To my Lord Jesus Christ, who encourages me to trust in Him, (Proverbs 3:5-6)

My father, Warren I. Robinson II (1941-2002), whose entrepreneurial spirit and encouraging words, "follow your dreams" helps me to go beyond my comfort zone

My mother, Kathleen Y. Robinson, who has blessed me with her creative vision and Christian inspiration

My sister, Cozette Y. Pettigrew, who is the backbone of my organization

My sister, Annette Y. Robinson, who is my advocate

My brothers, Warren I Robinson III and Darryl D. Robinson who always give their support

My best buddy (you know who you are) for always being there

The therapists of PYR Services for their love and dedication

To all the parents and caregivers who continuously inspire me

E. Madeline Morgan, for her commitment in the creation of this guidebook

This entire venture was a collaborative effort, I am so grateful for everyone who assisted me

22710606R00049

Printed in Great Britain
by Amazon